Guardian Angels

One Man's Experiences

TONY CARNESECCHI

ISBN 978-1-63903-151-1 (paperback)
ISBN 978-1-63903-152-8 (digital)

Christian Faith Publishing, Inc.
832 Park Avenue
Meadville, PA 16335
www.christianfaithpublishing.com

Printed in the United States of America

This book is dedicated to my loved ones, deceased and alive.

Guardian Angel Prayer

Angel of God, my guardian dear, to whom God's love commits me here, ever this day be at my side, to light, to guard, to rule and guide. Amen.

-Foreword-

I first started believing in guardian angels in the year of 1996, and this is what lead me to believe that my father intervened to save me when I was about to drown in boot camp. Here is what led me to believe.

My father-in-law was a very good man; family always came first with him, and he was the kind of caring man that would give you the shirt off his back. He'd help you out any way that he could. He was a bricklayer by trade, and he always worked hard. He set the example for his own sons and daughters so they would also grow up to be responsible hard-working adults too. I knew this fine man for longer than I knew my own dad; I always referred to him as dad when I spoke to him.

In the year of 1996, he became ill, and he'd shrugged it off as a bad cold. He was the type of man who would never go to see a doctor, no matter how bad he felt. A few weeks had gone by, and his illness was getting worse. With the suggestions from my mother-in-law, my wife, Sandi, and me that he needed to go to the doctor now, he still refused to go. It had gotten to the point where he couldn't even get out of bed and wasn't eating.

Finally, against his wishes, my mother-in-law called for an ambulance to come get him and take him to the ER where he was admitted to the hospital. It turned out, after many tests, that he had an inoperable tumor in his esophagus. He would spend the next weeks in a hospital bed, and I remember one evening, he asked me to get him a glass of water, but the doctor gave us strict instruction that he was not allowed to drink anything at the time. I felt so bad having to refuse his request. I couldn't do anything to help him.

Eventually, his condition would become worse to the point where they were giving him morphine to try and keep him as comfortable as was possible. His breathing would also become quickened as it would if he were running a marathon. Eyes closed, he would remain in this state for a while yet.

One evening and in to the early morning while visiting him, I decided to walk down the hall to the visitor's lounge. It was just a few doors down from his room, and I needed to just get out and go sit in there. It was about 2 a.m.; my mother-in-law, brothers-in-law, sister-in-law, and my wife stayed with him in his room. Everyone had fallen asleep with the exception of my wife, who sat by the side of his bed, holding his hand as he continued to breathe quickly. I sat down on the couch in the lounge, which was facing the doorway to the lounge. The television was on, but I really couldn't care what was on it; I paid no attention to it. I could hear the nurses talking at the nurse's station right outside the room. I decided to close my eyes for a bit, and that's when the vision appeared to me.

It was of a human form lying in a bed, and the form was made up of flames as though it was struggling, fighting a terrible battle. Hovering over that figure was an angel all dressed in white with a flowing gown, grabbing the figure's arm and gently pulling it upward. Then I heard a voice say, "Tony, Dad just passed away." It was Sandi standing in the doorway, and I looked at my watch. It was only 2:02 a.m.

I said, "I know. I just witnessed it." Only two minutes had passed from the time I went into the lounge and then. I was awake the whole time; I explained to my wife the vision I had just seen, and she told me of her own experience.

My father-in-law had ceased the quick breathing, and his breathing had become relaxed and normal. He opened his eyes, which he hadn't done for days. She told him that she loved him. And she said that it was as though he was looking right through her as if at someone else, and he had a slight grin on his face. Then he passed.

I told our pastor what I had seen in my vision, and he told me that I was privileged that I had gotten to see it, to reassure me of my beliefs. For many months after, I would close my eyes and concentrate on that vision, but I could never see it again. It had done its miracle.

I miss that man very much.

Perhaps you have had a similar experience.

I hope this book will open your mind and give you somewhat of a different perspective on your outlook of the possibilities of multiple guardian angels in your life through my experiences.

May God bless you.

CHAPTER ONE

-A Brief Biography-

Growing up as a young boy on the south side of Chicago in the area of Central Park Boulevard, Independence Avenue, Taylor Street, and Ogden Avenue was very special at that time between 1951 and 1961. It was mostly an Italian neighborhood back then; seemed like everyone knew each other. You could walk anywhere and also play anywhere and feel safe all the while. Many of my relatives also lived in the area, so we got to visit often; also got to see cousins frequently. One of my favorite memories is of my uncle Jerry's homemade Italian lemonade stand he would have on weekends. The *best* Italian lemonade I've ever had! As a young boy, it was a special time in my life. But it would eventually end in 1961 when our dad decided to move our family out to a northwest suburb, Rolling Meadows, which seemed to be so far away from where we were living on the south side of Chicago. I guess I would term it a desolate place back then. I was only ten years old at the time, so it seemed as though we were moving to another country!

There were five of us siblings; me being the youngest. This move was probably harder on my two brothers as they were fourteen and fifteen years old, and they had to leave many friends behind. My twin sisters were twelve years old; it may not have been so hard for them. I really don't remember. We moved into a house—something I don't remember us having in Chicago. My dad's sister and her husband and my cousin lived down the street from us there, so at least we had some family near us. And my cousin and I were only one year apart in age, he being older, so we hung out a lot together. I remember Mom hanging laundry on the clothesline outside. Mom would also fill up a large water basin so we could sit in it to cool off in the summertime. That was our pool.

As time went by, Dad decided to get into coaching little league. My cousin and I both were on the team. He was one of our pitchers, and I played left field. I was a pretty good fielder but couldn't hit very well. Dad never pressured me for that; he always said, "Don't worry. It'll come." It never came though; I just couldn't get the time down. As years went by, I realized that I was built for speed and strength. I gave up baseball, and in seventh and eighth grade, I was beating everyone in track at our school. That's when I knew I'd be signing up for the track team in high school.

In the school year 1966, I was in my eighth grade. It was a typical school year with the usual classes and lots of friends. But that year would become the worst, most devastating year I could ever imagine. Dad had contracted lung cancer, and he spent most of his days in bed in his bedroom, suffering with the terrible disease. Mom would take care of him as best as she could, but it was very hard on her because she also had five kids to tend to. Such sad times back then. I regret not going in my dad's room to visit him in his last days. The doctors had given him six months to live, and I guess I didn't want to believe it. I guess I always hoped that he would get better. One day in school, I was called to the principal's office, and my teacher walked with me to his office. I think I knew what this was about, but all the way down that hallway, I kept hoping it was for some other reason. When we got to his office and went in, he told me to have a seat; he had bad news for me. Dad had passed away—the worst news I could've ever gotten. I didn't want to believe it. His heart had given up beating; he was only fifty-six years old. I'd never get to say goodbye; I'd never get to hug him again; we'd never get to play catch again.

Mom was left with five kids now—fourteen-, sixteen-, eighteen-, and nineteen-year-olds. We all worked together now. Mom was going to need all of us to help her now. We would find jobs to help her out, and the man who owned a gas station down the road on Kirchoff Road knew we needed the money, so he took me on to fix flat tires, change tires, and pump gas (nobody pumped their own gas back then). We all managed, and it helped Mom out. I would move on eventually to work at the Rolling Meadows movie theater as an usher with my cousin Joe. His mom ran the ticket office. From there, I'd move on to the Rolling Meadows bowling alley. On my junior and senior year in high school, in the summers, I'd work at Wrigley Field and Falls on Sundays when the Bears played there. I always thought about Dad and how much I missed him. Nothing would ever be the same anymore, and Mom did the best she could. It was extremely hard on her.

I found out that Dad had requested Mom to get me a drum set the year that he passed away. So using some of Dad's insurance money, she surprised me with the drum set. His last gift to me, or so he thought. It's 2021 now, and I still have the drum set. I'll never let that part of him go. Although I haven't played it for the last ten years, I know it's here, and I know that he knows how much it means to me. I was self-taught, and the first song I learned on that drum set was "Wipe Out" by the Surfaris. That got me into a band, and we used to take turns practicing many songs in our garages. We got good enough that we began playing at the Park District's outdoor dances in the summer on Friday nights. It was fun times, and I'm sure Dad was proud. I remember my twin sisters, Jeanne and Joanie, and our neighbor, Joanne, dancing in our driveway as we played. It brought some happiness to an otherwise difficult situation. Maybe Dad knew that's what that drum set would do. So there's a somewhat brief biography.

CHAPTER TWO

-My First Experience-

In that fall of 1966, I was a freshman in high school. A newbie in a large high school—Forest View in Arlington Heights, Illinois. There were more kids in that school than I imagined there would be, and it was somewhat overwhelming to me. Of course the upperclassmen wanted nothing to do with you, and the nickname of "newbie" would describe all of us freshman as we would walk past them in the halls. It wasn't easy to make new friends, and losing Dad earlier in the year made it even harder for me. But gradually, I would make some. We all hung together, and eventually Mom would agree to me joining sports teams. A new and exciting experience for me! Football, track, and gymnastics practices would be at the end of the classes every day. Eventually I would get a job working at the Rolling Meadows bowling alley, where I would watch the pin-setting machines and the people bowling, and when one of those machines would jam up, I'd have to run to the back and set a pin or more up so that person could continue. Me and the other guy who worked with me would take turns when needed and also watch for any trouble in the bowling alley, which would happen sometimes in the summer months when we'd get workers from the Arlington Park horse racing track would come to the bar there and get drunk. We'd immediately call the police in if they'd get rowdy.

There was a girl from high school who worked in the snack bar there, and she would always have a pizza and a vanilla milkshake with an egg in it ready for me when I got to work. It was an okay job, and the money I would make would go to help Mom out; that was the most important part of it. I would be done by 10:00 p.m. and head home to go to bed. I did this for my freshman and sophomore years. Classes, sports practice, work, and then home.

Over my high school years, I would go on to compete in all three of the sports, but track was my favorite. I was in several events in track, and in my senior year, running the 440-yard dash was my specialty. I had the chance to go downstate in that event if I could get my time down to fifty seconds. My current time in that event was 51.4 seconds, so I had to knock off 1.4 seconds. I felt confident. I worked hard training for four years, and this would be my best run! I knew all of the other guys on my teams had the advantage of going home to a nice dinner after practice and then get to do any home-work or studying they had. I'd have to do mine during study hall in school. I guess this fact gave me more incentive to give this race my all. I practiced harder and always had the best 440 times in our school that senior year.

It was time for the race to start after waiting for a large part of the day, doing stretches, warming up, wind sprints, and having lots of butterflies in my stomach with the anticipation of what was to come. I had many high school friends in the stands all wishing me luck and cheering me on. My two sisters and two brothers were not there because of their own activities, and Mom was never at any of my events because she didn't drive and had no way of making them. Four hard years of training and hard work, and I was going to try my hardest to make it all pay off on this day—this one race. We were all at our staggered starting points as we waited for the starting gun to sound off.

"Ready, set..." *Bang!* The time had finally come. We were off and running. I had a good pace going, breathing was good, I felt good about this. Out of a field of seven guys from different high schools, I was in third place as we approached the final turn; but I was close to the first and second place guys. We came out of that turn pretty even, and I knew it was time for me to kick in all the energy I had left, so that's what I did. As we all raced to the finish line, I crossed first! I thought for sure that I had done it—qualified to go downstate. This was the best I had ever run. I knew I had broken my best time of 51.4 seconds, but did I break it enough? When the final times were announced, in first place from Forest View High School was Tony Carnesecchi at 50.6 seconds! I was so disappointed, six-tenths of one second! I didn't qualify because somewhere along the race, I only needed to knock off 0.6 seconds more! It was beyond my comprehension, and I couldn't imagine what more I could've done. My only consolation was that I won the race, and all the guys were congratulating each other and glad that we had that chance and ran our hearts out. Over the years, I learned to appreciate that fact more and realized that there are so many more important things in life. I look back now and remember so many fun times of it all.

Dad never got to see me in any of my high school sports events, or at least that's what I thought back then. Later I would come to believe that Dad was most likely watching, cheering me on, smiling and proud.

In my junior and senior years of high school, 1969 and 1970, I was fortunate to get a job at Wrigley Field, managing the right field upper deck concession, where only vendors would come to pick up whatever refreshments and food they were selling that day. It was mostly popcorn, peanuts, Coke, and beer. The summers consisted of working the Cubs games when they were in town, and back then, the Bears also played there during football season, so I also got to be there for every game. I worked with two other people in that stand, so once we got everything set up, I was able to stand outside and watch all the games. It was the most fun job back then, even though it was low-paying. Dad was a huge Cubs fan, and he was probably very happy that I could work there.

In 1970, I was standing down by the upper deck railing in the front row, by the first base line. Back then, you could watch the players' warm ups, and I decided to bring my glove with me one day. As the Hall of Famer Ernie Banks, a Cubs legend, was doing some warm-ups, I decided to yell down to him, "Hey, Ernie, toss one up to me!" And to my surprise, he did! We played catch that way for a few minutes, then it was time for fielding practice to begin. What a fun experience for me, playing catch with Mr. Cub! He was always a fun, jovial man who loved the game. His motto would be "Let's play two!" I think he would've played a double-header every day if he could've. It was quite the honor to play catch with baseball greatness! Many years later at an autograph session at a sports event, I had the pleasure to meet him again and shake hands and get my photo taken with him. I thought I would mention to him about that time we played catch at Wrigley with him throwing a ball back and forth to the kid in the upper deck.

"Oh man, that was you?" he remembered and said so many fun and good memories from back then, in his playing years. I also got the team to autograph a baseball for me in 1969, the year that we all thought we'd be in the World Series. That was a huge disappointment too!

One day after the Cubs game was over and all of the spectators had left, clean-up ended, and a group of us guys had decided to play around on the field, hitting balls to each other, running around the bases, etc.... I was batting while one of the guys would pitch the ball from in front of the pitching mound. I think my four years as a ringman in gymnastics had paid off on this one—strong arms and shoulders. And as the ball was pitched to me, I jacked one into the third row of the left field bleachers! I trotted around the bases, waving my arms and yelling, "Oh yeah, he got all of that one!" What fun times back then. Dad would've loved it!

The school year ended. I graduated and worked my last summer at Wrigley Field. As they say, all good things come to an end, and sadly, this was one of those things. I believe that Dad was there to see it all.

We could in no way afford college, so I decided to follow in Dad's footsteps and join the navy. I entered on the second of November 1970 (ironically, the Cubs would win the World Series on November 2, forty-six years later). We were given dungarees, caps, skivvies (undershorts we had to put our names on), socks, shower shoes and boots, and a needle and thread to hem our own pants.

There were eighty-eight guys in my boot camp company barracks from all around the country. You'd hear all sorts of things as you were trying to sleep at night. Great Lakes Naval Base in November is a pretty cold place to be, and we marched to every class, every training drill, and every meal for eight weeks. We were actually in for ten weeks due to a two-week quarantine from spinal meningitis in our company. Our educational petty officer died from it.

You had to wash your own clothes on a scrub board and hang them outside using clothes stops, not clothes pins. Clothes stops are short pieces of rope you'd use to tie the ends of your pant legs and shirt sleeves to the line. And you had to do this every night in your T-shirt, boxers, and shower shoes. Then go out in the morning at 5:00 a.m. to take your stiff clothes off the line, let them thaw so you could fold them, and put them in your locker; and they better be put away neatly! Shine your boots so that you could see your reflection in them. Make up your rack (bed) with hospital corners and make it tight so a quarter could bounce off of it!

We had different flags that your company could win and carry while the company marched everywhere. There were competitions to win these flags. We won the athletic flag every week, and I believe we won the educational flag five of eight weeks. Friday nights would get boring, so I decided to enter the Friday night boxing matches for something to do. We always had to wear those protective headgear soft helmets. I went and signed up at the drill hall where they were held. In eight weeks, I lost three times, but never got knocked out though. Like I said, something to do, and it helped to keep me in shape.

We went through several things in boot camp including being locked in a room, five of us at a time, with a tear gas mask. Tear gas would be filtered through vents, and you had to hold your mask until you were ordered to put it on. That wouldn't come until you were at the point where you could no longer hold your breath or you couldn't see very well. Great time!

But my first near-death experience would come at a different test. This test was the swimming survival test. For this test, you'd dip your pants in the pool to get them wet, then tie the ends of each leg into a knot. You'd hold them over your head, and then, as you jumped into the pool, you'd swing them over your head. And as the legs would fill up with air, you would slap the waist onto the water and put one inflated leg under each arm. Then you'd wade across the pool. And this worked very well, except if the guy next to you would lose one of his legs and panic because he wasn't a good swimmer! And that's precisely what happened to me—the guy who was next to me had it happen to him, and he panicked. I was treading along fine until I felt him grab onto me, and he managed to wrap his legs under each armpit of mine. I took a real deep breath as I sunk to the bottom of the pool, and I could hear him above water yelling for help! His legs were locked on me like two vice grips as I held my breath and struggled to get free from the grasp while he was sitting on my shoulders. Fortunately, I was in very good shape and could hold my breath for a long time. I struggled as much as I could, but his adrenalin was working overtime. I could see my life pass before my eyes as I was running out of oxygen, and I had to let the air out as slowly as I could watching the air bubbles floating up. I remember thinking, *Dear God, don't let me die this way.* The last bit of air was about to be exhaled when I saw two lifeguards coming underwater to free me from those vice grips that held me under for so long. They got us loose from each other, and one of them swam me over to the side of the pool and helped me out of the water, and I proceeded to vomit and collapse trying to catch my breath. This is where I believe my first encounter with my guardian angel occurred, and I believe it was my dad. He would not have wanted me to end this way.

CHAPTER THREE

---　✳　---

-Code Blue-

My time in the navy, four years, was interesting to say the least. After boot camp, I received my orders, stating that I was to attend the Naval Hospital Corpsman Training School at the Great Lakes, Illinois, training facility. It was determined from my testing that I would make a good hospital corpsman (medic). I had no idea what this would encompass, but I got my orders, and I had to follow them. One thing you learned in the military was responsibility, not just for yourself, but also for your fellow brothers and sisters who were serving.

The training was extremely intense; it was basically two years of nursing school crammed into four months! We would learn as much as possible to prepare us for our duty, and then learn even more as we got our next orders. School was all day, and then you'd have to study until very late in the evenings, usually until around midnight. Then you'd get maybe four or five hours of shuteye and then up to do it again, day after day, for four months.

We learned everything from the *PDR* (*Physicians' Desk Reference*), where we'd have to study prescription drugs, their uses, their formal names, how to spell them, how to give shots, anatomy and physiology, and everything in between! Tests would come once a week every Friday, and you had better pass the test, or you were out of corps school and reassigned to a different duty. Unfortunately, there were a few guys who couldn't cut it. The Vietnam War was raging, and there was no time for failure.

After I completed corps school, my first tour of duty was on a neurosurgical ward at the Great Lakes Naval Hospital, where more training would take place. I would be trained by nurses who were officers on how to maintain a patient's medical chart, how to take rectal temperature, how to disinfect a comatose patient, how to suction a tracheotomy tube, etc.—so many aspects of nursing that we didn't learn in the corps school. This ward consisted of paraplegics, quadriplegics, and comatose patients. These were guys from the ages of eighteen to twenty-three years old who entered the military in perfectly good health but would sustain injuries such as these that would change their lives forever.

After months of on-the-job training, I would be assigned to one patient in a room by himself whom I had to care for my entire shift, whether it be days, evenings, or nights. Eight hours with one guy. He was a twenty-one-year-old demolitions guy in Vietnam. I'll never forget him. David White was his name. Apparently, he had gotten hit in the front of his head by a rock as he was blowing up an area.

Surgery would remove the frontal lobe of his brain. He could no longer fend for himself. He had a tracheotomy tube with an oxygen machine attached to it and three decubitus bedsores—one on each hip and his coccyx bone area—that formed in the hospital in Japan where he was originally transported to. These bedsores form from the lack of repositioning the patient every few hours. His sores were too bad to ever heal; you could see bone, as there was a silver-dollar-sized opening where the skin and all underlying tissues had worn away. All we could do now was put dressings on them and make sure I turned him every few hours. He also had a feeding tube inserted into his stomach where a type of protein milkshake mixture would hang on an IV stand and slowly drain into his stomach. I won't go into the rest of the details, but I came to consider David a good friend; and I would do all that I could for him, whether it was reading to him or talking to him about the day's events whether he could understand me or not. I just wanted to let him know that he wasn't alone. His mom and dad would come from Michigan every weekend to visit him. His fiancée came for some time also, but she knew he would never get any better, so she eventually stopped coming.

After eight months of taking care of David, he would be transferred to Hines VA Hospital in River Grove, Illinois, where he would pass away only a few weeks later, I learned. I was pretty sad about that.

I received a letter of commendation from the Secretary of the Navy for outstanding care and treatment of David White. I was honored, and I know Dad would've been proud of me.

I had a few other duties within my four years: I got to deliver a baby along with my partner when I was stationed in a dispensary. We were called one night, so we jumped in our ambulance and headed over to the apartment where this lady lived along with her husband and five other kids. By the time we got there, her water bag had already broken, and she was ready. We had no choice! It went pretty smoothly, and we clamped the umbilical cord, wrapped the baby girl up, and let the mother hold her to her chest as we loaded them onto the stretcher and transported them to the hospital with me sitting in the back of the ambulance with her. That was the best experience I had in my four years of duty.

In between those four years, I got married to Sandi, my wife of forty-nine years now, and we had our first child, a daughter, Tammy Rene, in 1972. I finished my military stint in September of 1974. All in all, it was quite an experience that when I think back, I'd most likely do it all again.

As the years went by, we had our second and final child, a son we named Jason Anthony, in 1977, five years after our daughter. Our kids were a joy, and they still are! Our family was complete now, and eventually they would both marry and give us two grandkids each— one boy and three girls. We love them all so much.

My mom passed away in 1984. She had a pretty hard life, and it was even harder when Dad passed away eighteen years earlier. Mom did the best she could over those years. She ended up getting employment at some factory where she'd be an assembler for years. During those eighteen years, she'd have bouts with cancer on and off in various parts of her body, but I don't remember her ever complaining about any of it. I do remember driving her to her chemo treatments, and sometimes she would cry on the ride home. She went through a lot and would eventually end up in a hospice center. I remember one evening, Sandi and I were visiting her, and suddenly she looked away from us and to a different part of her room where she began talking in Italian while staring at that area. I finally asked her who she was talking to.

She looked at me and said, "Someday you'll find out."

We stayed and visited for a while longer, then we were told by the nurse that it was time for us to leave. We kissed Mom and said our goodbyes. That was the last time we would see her alive, as she passed away the following day.

She was a trooper for all those years and all the problems she had, but I think Dad had come to get her. Another angel had gone home.

In 1978, we bought a cute little cocker spaniel puppy, and we named her Buffy. She was a joy to have, and our kids loved her; she was a great companion to us all. Christmas would be such fun for all the years we had her, and she was a good girl all those years. She grew up with our children, was fun-loving, and did what dogs do. Our children were six years and one year old at the time, so growing up together meant so much to them. Buffy lived for fifteen and a half years before her passing in 1993. It was a sad time for all of us, and there was a great void in our family. Our children eventually asked if we could get another dog. So after six weeks, we finally agreed to get another dog. This time, it was a yellow Labrador retriever. My wife and kids went to pick her out. I remember when I came from work; they were all out in the yard. My daughter's boyfriend had gone with them, and he ended up getting a black Lab too! I saw them in the yard and went out to see this new pup. She was a little runt! Have you ever seen a puppy whose head was bigger than its body? I was expecting a little roly-poly, but she was the runt of the litter, under-fed. It wouldn't take long; by the next day, she was my buddy. My wife wanted to name her Samantha, so we always called her Sam or Sammy. What a sweetie she was! Very intelligent, loving, playful, and very affectionate.

She was so easy to train too; it was as if she knew what I wanted her to do. Training school was very easy with her. She was very well behaved, never did her business in the house, never chewed on anything except her toys and of course Christmas wrappings! It turned out that she was born on the same day that we had to let Buffy pass. The date was on her birth certificate. I never thought it was a coincidence, as occasionally, I would call her Buffy to see her reaction. She would stop whatever she was doing and turn to look at me, ears up and tail wagging. You know those butt wiggles that dogs get? Like she knew! We had an aboveground swimming pool in the yard, and Jason and I would run around the perimeter of the oval pool, and Sammy would chase us.

Sometimes she'd stop halfway around, reverse her field, and come around to catch us in front. It was quite fun for all of us. She loved the pool, would swim around, and dive underwater to fetch her solid rubber ball that would sink to the bottom. And she loved the float! I would lift her up onto it and pull her around the pool, and when she'd get too hot, she would just fall into the water again. Many, many days of summer fun with her. She was so much fun year round! She was the best, and she also lived fifteen and a half years, passing away in 2008. It was an extremely sad event—the fourth angel had crossed over. I still miss that girl every day. It took us ten years after her passing to get another dog that I rescued—an Australian shepherd / border collie mix that I named Liberty. She's three years old now, extremely intelligent and affectionate, and we love her.

It was Easter morning, 2009. I began to feel pain in both of my forearms and hands. Have you ever experienced a severe toothache? That's what it felt like, and I wondered what could be causing it? This was not any kind of symptoms of a heart attack that I knew of, but I couldn't think of anything else. I told my wife to drive me to the emergency room, as St. Joseph Hospital is only three blocks away, a straight shot. This may sound foolish to some of you, but by the time we would call for an ambulance and they'd arrive, check my vitals, and load me onto their stretcher to transport me to the hospital, we'd have already been there and checked into the emergency room. When we arrived at the hospital, I told my wife to drop me off at the door and go park the car, I walked in and told the nurse at the desk that I thought I was having a heart attack. Have any of you ever experienced these symptoms before? Or for those of you who may have had a heart attack, have you had any of the traditional symptoms?

The nurse got a wheelchair and wheeled me into the ER, and I got onto one of their beds. They hooked up an EKG machine and drew some blood while my wife, Sandi, sat beside the bed. The ER doctor came over and asked me what was the problem, and I told him that I was having a heart attack.

"What are your symptoms? Chest pain, shortness of breath, etc.?"

I told him, "No, none of those typical symptoms. Just pain in both forearms and hands."

He told me my EKG looked fine and that we'd have to wait for my blood results to come back.

I told him that as a medic, I've taken very many EKGs, and they don't always show what's going on, so I don't put much faith in them.

A little time went by, and then I heard over the speaker in the ER, "Code blue!"

The nurse came over to my bed and I said, "It sounds like someone's in trouble."

She said, "That's for you. We want to make sure everyone gets to the OR and is ready to receive you for an angiogram."

The doctor came over to tell me that I was having a heart attack, and I told him, "That's what I've been telling you all since I walked in here!" Only about twenty to twenty-five minutes had passed since I walked into the ER to when they wheeled me into the OR for the angiogram.

The angiogram was done, and a balloon was inserted until I would have the surgery two days later once my heart muscles firmed up again. Dr. Steimle was raised on a farm, and you'd never guess that by looking at her or talking to her that she was one of the best heart surgeons in the Fox Valley area. It turned out that her two daughters used to attend our Kids Summer Art Camps at my art studio! Small world indeed, and she would perform five bypasses and install a mechanical aorta valve (made in Italy). By the way, I reference the mechanical aorta valve because I'm Italian. It was sort of a funny coincidence in an eight-hour operation that morning!

I was put into an induced coma, and later that night or very early morning, I would have complications. My blood pressure would drop to 60/40, and my wife told me that I was very pale and swollen. Dr. Steimle was called as my sisters, son, and best friend had all come in. Apparently, they all thought that I wasn't going to survive that night, but Dr. Steimle reassured them all that she was not going to let me die after all of the work she performed on me that morning. Sandi also kept positive thoughts that I would pull through this setback. It turned out that a drainage tube had been leaking, and blood was pooling up in my chest cavity. Dr. Steimle took me back down to the OR, opened me up again, and cleaned me out, fixed me up, and closed me back up. She doesn't close by doing sutures, she uses a resin glue. It's ugly, turns black, and takes over a month to all fall off.

I spent nine days in the CICU, five of those I don't remember. Once I left there, it was up into a ward for recuperation and some rehab. It's amazing how much muscle control you can lose in those nine days lying in a bed. I had machines almost wall to wall with twenty-one IVs going at once! I had a breathing tube down my throat and a catheter. The induced coma would be beneficial at that time! Have any of you been laid up so long that you had to learn how to walk again and swallow again? Yes, I couldn't get out of CICU until I could do those two things. I can't explain the hallucinations during my time in the induced coma, but I do know that I was not alone.

After a week on the ward and a total of sixteen days in the hospital, actually eighteen because of the two days they waited for my heart muscle to firm up, I was finally allowed to go home where I would spend two more months recuperating before I could finally return to my art studio and teach classes again. Sandi was by my side this entire time, worrying and praying.

Things were getting back to normal again. I often wondered what prompted me to believe I was having a heart attack. During the time from first experiencing the pain in my forearms and hands until the angiogram, why were there no other symptoms in those twenty to twenty-five minutes? What prevented me from going into cardiac failure when I had complications later that night?

I believe this was the second intervention by my dad, mom, Buffy, Sammy, and if you believe living angels exist, Sandi.

CHAPTER FOUR

-Listen to Your Doctor-

The year 2010 would prove to be yet another dark, depressing, and sad one. When you grow up with four other siblings who are all older than you, you tend to look up to them; and when two of them are your older brothers, you sometimes try to emulate them. I had twin sisters, Jean and Joan, who are two years older than me, and I had two older brothers, Mick who was four years older, and Vito who was five years older. Yes, I am the baby of us five siblings. I suppose that had some good advantages such as "Stop picking on your little brother" and "One of you must've taught him that." I'm sure some of you can relate to that. But there were also some disadvantages, like not being included in certain things or activities that your siblings did.

My brothers and I all shared a bedroom. We had a set of bunk beds, and being the youngest, I'd get the top bunk. Many nights, I would pretend to be asleep as I would listen to my brothers talk about their dates and things. I suppose I learned some things from those "spy" sessions!

As the years passed by, Mick, whom I always felt closest to, moved to Michigan with his family, and we would form a bond. We would stay in contact by phone, and occasionally Sandi and I would go there to visit; and he would come with his wife and kids to visit by us. Like myself, Mick was a huge Chicago Cubs fan. We'd go to some

Cubs games with a few of his sons and sons-in-law, and one year with my brother, Vito. We had some fun times back then, but mostly it was weekly phone calls.

Mick had diabetes, and it became very bad over years of struggling with it. Some of you may know what I mean. As much as he tried to control it, it would become futile for him. He contracted a cancer that could not be treated with chemotherapy; therefore, radiation treatments were the only option. One of the major problems with radiation treatments is that it can affect other internal organs. That's precisely what would happen to Mick, as eventually he would begin to have bleeding problems. His doctors would never really get it under control. Even though they would locate a bleed and cauterize that area, another area would eventually begin to bleed. Over time, it would take many trips to the hospital for blood transfusions as the bleeding began to take over. Poor Mick went through so much over this period, and his wife, Ellen, took care of him as best she could. His urine and stool became mostly blood, and after months of suffering and transfusions, it would finally take his life.

I'll always remember our last visit to see him. When Sandi and I were leaving to head home to Illinois, we gave each other hugs as much as Mick's condition would allow and kissed each other on the cheek and said "I love you" to each other. We both knew that this would be the last time we'd see each other as tears welled up.

After the long battle with this terrible disease, Mick passed away in May of 2010. He fought a long hard battle, enduring much more suffering than anyone should have to. He remained strong-willed to the end. I miss him every day, and yes, I tell him so every day.

The fifth guardian angel had arrived.

After many months through the summer and fall of mourning Mick's passing, my art studio would keep me occupied, and it was good to have my students, whom I considered to be my friends, near me over these months.

My brother-in-law, George, was the best brother-in-law a guy could have. He was a few years older than me, and I always considered George more of a brother than a brother-in-law. He was married to my sister Jeanne, and they lived nearby. It was always enjoyable when we'd get together. George was also an ex-navy guy, and when he got discharged, he spent most of his post-navy time as a carpenter, which he was very good at; and George was the type of guy who would help you when needed. He'd give you the shirt off his back, as the saying goes. And he had one of those laughs that was contagious—the type of laugh where you'd laugh along with him even if you didn't even know what he was laughing about! As years went by, we would end up working together; we were also teammates on a bowling league team. It was always fun times when we'd visit Jeanne and George.

I remember one time when the drywall on part of the ceiling in my garage had started to sag. This was shortly after my heart attack and when I was still recovering, so I won't able to go up on a ladder to screw it back up. George came over to do it for me; he was glad to help. Another time, he had come to help me install a new front-entry door on our house. Like I said, he was always willing to help where he could. Eventually, he would build a new home for Jeanne and him. It was a beautiful ranch home, large with a full basement. Years went by, and when the tragedy of 9/11 happened, the building trades took a very hard hit in this area; and George had rough times finding companies to work for, as many builders and developers in the area were forced to close. As a few years passed, George ended up getting a job at a Siegel's store here—a retail and building supplier. We both worked for them as building estimators, a very decent job.

George had developed a heart condition, but he would refuse to get an angiogram, partly due to seeing what I had gone through. He would eventually have a heart attack. We got the call one night from Jeanne that he was in an ambulance being transported to the ER at Sherman Hospital. Jean was following and I could meet her there. I was in my car in no time, heading over to the hospital that is only a mile away, so it didn't take me long. When I got there, doctors and nurses were already trying to revive George. I sat there with Jeanne and watched them do everything they could to bring him back, shock paddles, etc.... They would finally get a heartbeat, but he remained unconscious, as the lack of oxygen to his brain had been about fifteen minutes. He was admitted to CICU, where he would never recover, and he passed away a few weeks later on Christmas Eve of 2010. Another devastating loss and guardian angel number 6 had arrived. I miss that laugh.

In 2014, five years after my heart attack, I noticed some blood in my stool, but I ignored it for a week or so, figuring it was a bleeding hemorrhoid. It didn't let up though and began to get worse. To those of you who've experienced this, did you ever have any indigestion or stomachaches with it? I did not. My primary doctor had recommended that I should get a colonoscopy done many months prior to this happening since I was beyond the fifty years old age recommendation. But I had kept putting it off until this problem prompted me into getting one done.

The gastroenterologist came to see me after the procedure was done, after I had become coherent, to talk to me and explain that I had a tumor in my large intestine the size of a golf ball, and I would be needing surgery to remove it—something I never wanted to hear. But I felt confident that I would be fine. One or more of my guardian angels would see to it. It turned out that I had to have a foot of my colon removed, but the tumor had not attached itself to any other part of my colon, and all lymph nodes proved to be clear of any cancer. The surgeon said that I should be the poster boy for those who have a large tumor in the colon that wasn't attached to any other part and left everything else clean and cancer-free. It was extremely unusual, and it was referred to as superficial cancer. No chemotherapy was needed. Relief was an understatement, but recovery was compared to a woman in labor for five days—extremely painful and uncomfortable, but a very small price to pay. My guardian angels are awesome!

This would be the third intervention—Dad, Mom, Buffy, Sammy, Mick, and George? Can we have more than one guardian angel? Can our beloved pets who were also family members be guardian angels too?

Do you believe yet, or do you think that I've just been lucky? I've had some really great surgeons, but sometimes it takes more than a great surgeon. Read on…

CHAPTER FIVE

-My Loyal Friends-

I'm going to digress to the year 1967 here, to introduce you to a fun, beautiful girl who would eventually become my sister-in-law. Her name is Joanne, and she would be an awesome sister-in-law.

But years before that would happen, I was the drummer in a rock and roll band that some friends had formed, and we'd practice in the garage at each other's houses. When we'd practice in the garage at my house, my twin sisters Jean and Joan, along with Joanne, would sometimes dance on our driveway when we played. We were pretty good too; we'd play at the outdoor Friday night dances and a few sock hops in the school gymnasium. Those were some fun times. There was a place called the Cellar in Arlington Heights where real good bands would play. There was a band named the Shadows of Night, who would play there and would go on to make a rock and roll hit called "Gloria," which is one of two songs I was allowed to sing in our band while I played the drums to it. We named our band a sort of take-off of the Shadows of Night. We called ourselves the Lords of Darkness. I even painted our name on the front skin of my bass drum, à la the Beatles! It was cool!

My brother Vito would start dating Joanne, and they would date for many years until they'd finally marry. They'd go on to have two sons, Anthony (who was named after me) and Joseph (who was named after Joanne's father). Anthony is the same age of my son Jason, and visiting with Joanne and Vito was always a fun time. Holidays, Christmases, birthdays, we'd always have a good time; and even though Vito was five years older than I am, we always got along well.

As time went on, their son Anthony would get married, and his wife Melanie would give birth to a daughter, Elizabeth, a few years later. Joanne and Vito finally had a cute little granddaughter they loved beyond words. Joanne was in her glory, so happy, so proud to be a grandma.

I move on now to 2015. My sister Joan had gotten a divorce from her abusive husband many years prior, but they had two daughters in the early years of their marriage, Angela and Brenda. Two sweet girls who Joan would end up raising pretty much by herself and with not much financial support from her ex, who moved out of state and remarried. Joan never remarried. I guess maybe she had a hard time trusting another man enough. So she lived her life as a single mom, working and raising two kids and doing her best to try and make a decent life for her girls. It was never easy, and she had some bad breaks along the way, but she persevered, and her two girls would become two great wives and mothers of their own awesome children. Joan would have three grandsons whom she loved so much, and she would do anything for them. She, too, was a proud grandma. Over the years, Joan would have many setbacks, but through it all, she was always concerned for others. She'd always joke or act silly, jovial, extroverted, and everybody loved Joanie. She even took the time to come and watch over me as I was at home rehabilitating from my heart surgery while my wife Sandi was at work. She always did whatever she could to help others, never mind her own problems she may have been having.

Joan had contracted breast cancer and had a mastectomy. She had beaten this cancer and was so relieved, so happy, and back to her usual ways! But as the years passed, she would have to move from the condo she was renting to move in with one of her daughters and her family.

We all have cancer cells in our bodies, and it all depends on what activates them. Many years after beating her breast cancer, cancer returned to cause her to put up a terrible struggle, even worse than the first time. Eventually she would succumb, no matter what her doctors would try. In March of 2015, Joanie passed away. Sadly, another angel would join my other family members—she would be the seventh.

Too many losses in such a short period. There isn't a day that goes by that I don't think of them all, miss them all so much, and talk to them all. I'm confident that many of you can relate to this. We all carry on with our lives, don't we? They're always in our thoughts aren't they?

It was September 27, 2015—my birthday, and the day we would lose Joanne to stage 4 lung cancer. She battled for months with chemo; and while Vito took care of her as best he could and tried to make her comfortable, she was suffering mentally. She was only able to have her new granddaughter for about a year; something she probably missed the most. Another very tragic loss six months after the loss of Joanie. I knew Joanne since 1966—almost fifty years. I loved her like a sister now. Another angel, number 8, had joined the others.

I believe that guardian angels are there for you when you need them if you believe in them and their powers to help you. Can we have more than one guardian angel? I believe we can, depending on the situation where more help is needed.

September 1, 2016, would prove to be another tough experience for me. I think August 28 is when my headaches began. I've had severe migraines in the past, so severe that I'd have to go to the ER where they would have to inject morphine into me. Other times, my chiropractor would do a few adjustments on my neck, and that would do the trick! But these headaches were nothing like a migraine; they felt like just your normal headache, so I thought they'd just finally stop. I would be able to sleep at night, but the next morning, the headache would still be there. I'd be taking Tylenol, but it wasn't giving me any relief. Finally, after four days, I asked Sandi if she would drive me to the chiropractor as I really didn't feel like driving myself. So she did; we got there and went inside, but now I could feel myself getting weaker. I told the chiropractor what had been going on with my headaches, so she decided to take my blood pressure before even attempting any adjustments on me. It turned out that my blood pressure was 250/170!

She said, "There's obviously something going on, and Sandi needs to drive you over to the clinic."

We proceeded to go, but I told Sandi that I thought she should just drive me to the ER at St. Joe's Hospital instead. It was about five or six miles down Randell Road, and then a few quick blocks to the hospital. I began to get dizzy spells as we were driving there, which would cause me to vomit more than once while I hung my head out the window of the car, my new car. The weakness was getting worse, as was the vomiting as we arrived at the ER. Nurses came out and put me on a gurney and wheeled me in while Sandi went to park the car. As they pushed the gurney into an ER room, every turn they made made me vomit again. It got to the point where there was nothing left but dry vomiting now. They gave me an IV, attached heart monitoring to me, and gave me antinausea meds. I was in that ER room about an hour, and the headaches were worse now.

A CT scan was ordered for my brain, and they wheeled me to that room where it took three nurses to get me onto the CT scan table. I got the scan, then it was back to the ER room until the doctor could read my scan. The results showed a very large blood mass forming. I had been having a brain hemorrhage, and surgery would be coming very soon! I thought, *Okay, guys, I need your help again!*

My surgeon was an awesome Italian named Dr. Cascino. This man was different from the other surgeons I've had. I think he could see or sense my concern, so he walked alongside the gurney as they wheeled me to the OR, talking to me and reassuring me that everything would be fine. It was somewhat comforting knowing that he cared enough to do that instead of just waiting in the OR for me to arrive.

After a while in the recovery room, I woke up to see Sandi sitting by my side as she's always done. There was my sister Jean and a few others along with a few nurses. Now I know how a monkey must feel as he sees everyone staring at him! It was great to see everyone there. I remember thinking, *Thank you all again for seeing me through another very close call.* People there were talking to me, but I was still too groggy to answer them.

I was eventually moved up to a room on a ward, and friends and family would come to visit me. Even some of my adult students from my art studio would stop and cheer me up. It was so nice to see everybody.

After a few days on the ward, Dr. Cascino came in to check on me, see how I was doing and feeling. He told me that I owed him a pizza for the hard work he had done to save my life. He said that he wasn't sure that I'd make it on the OR table and that I had him scared, that it could've been the opposite. He told me that most people who experience headaches like that go to sleep and never wake back up, and how in hell did I make it that long? I told him that I had special help.

I now have a six-inch scar that goes up the back of my neck and head from eighteen metal staples. My guardian angels were working overtime for sure!

After a week on the ward, recuperating and waiting for the cut to heal so they could remove the staples, which I kept, I was transported just a block away to rehab center, where I would spend three weeks. It was a nice place with friendly staff, doctors, nurses, and physical and mental therapists—all very nice people. It was square with a very nice courtyard and gazebo in the center of it with nice plants and flowers and some veggies planted.

I was determined to do my rehab and get out and back home to Sandi and the studio. I did everything they wanted me to do, and some of it was extremely boring. I had to use a walker to get around, and it was difficult to make it down the hallway halfway, but I worked at it constantly until I no longer needed the walker, which took about a week. The distance of the length of each hall was posted at the beginning and end of each hall, and the halls were wide. Twenty laps around the square would equal two miles, which I would eventually get to! But in the beginning, as I was walking down the hall with my walker one day, I ran into two of my favorite students who were coming to visit me, Julie and Nikki. What a pleasant surprise that was! We went and sat in the gazebo and talked, and they stayed for quite a while. It was so great to see them. I enjoyed walking the halls a few times a day, meeting some of the other patients, talking with other patients, and just passing the time.

I finally got released to go home with restrictions, and I wasn't allowed to drive yet, but it was so good to be home again. For the next week, I'd have visiting nurses come to the house to check on me, take my vitals, etc.... I remember when they told me that I could return to the studio but not teach yet, and only for a few hours.

I'd go just to observe and say hi to everyone as my loyal employee Karen was covering my classes as she had done many times in the past for my other recoveries.

Through all of these incidents, my studio still remains, and I am still able to teach art.

If you believe that you can have more than one guardian angel, do they summon each other for help if the situation calls for more than one of them? I believe that's a possibility.

CHAPTER SIX

-My Guardian Angel's Working Hard-

Do guardian angels need a few seconds of warning of an impending tragedy before they can intervene?

In 2018, I had yet another devastating loss! My oldest brother, Vito, became the man of the family at age nineteen when Dad passed away. He would help Mom and us siblings as best he could. He was a hard worker, and eventually he would go to barber school and become a certified barber. With his pompadour hairstyle and his toughness, I always thought he was so cool, and I looked up to him. We had gotten a paper route for a while. He would drive the Pontiac Tempest slowly up and down the streets of the suburb we lived in, and I would sit on the trunk of the car with a sack of rolled up papers that we had prepared. And I would fling them onto the lawns or driveways of the people's houses. Occasionally he would let me drive it at only five or ten miles per hour, and that's how I learned to drive at age fourteen. Most of the money we'd make would go to help out mom.

I had started working at a neighborhood gas station during the summer when I was fourteen years old. That was when you actually pumped gas for customers, cleaned their windshield, checked the oil, and I'd occasionally repair flat tires. That was the extent of duties the owner allowed me to do. He was very nice to hire me on, and he knew we needed the money.

One day, I let Vito talk me into him giving me a haircut for practice. Unfortunately, I had to go to school with it! It was not very good. I had patches on my head; he laughed and told me, "It's not that bad!" He had a ways to go before he'd become a barber as far as I was concerned! When I look back on that time, I still chuckle. It was somewhat funny.

Vito was the last one of us five siblings to get married to Joanne. Over the years, we'd visit for various reasons, and we'd always stop by their house—Sandi and I with our children, either on Christmas or Christmas Eve. Our kids would play together, and it was always a nice visit.

Many years had passed, and Vito had gotten a job working for the state of Illinois in a maintenance position. And in the winters, he'd always hope for lots of snow so he could work overtime plowing; but he'd still work part time on Saturdays for a barbershop he was hired at. He was always trying to make more money so his family would never want for anything, and Joanne didn't have to work too.

But like my other brother, Mick, Vito had diabetes. And like Mick, he never really got it under control. They both had a sweet tooth and fought it for years. Eventually insulin injections every day would be needed like Mick and Mom. As time went on, the passing of Joanne really hurt him badly, and he would have so many regrets.

Then one day, one of his small toes on his left foot was turning black from him previously bumping it on something. He paid no attention to it and thought that it was just a bad bruise, but it finally blackened, and he went to have it checked out thanks to the insistence of my sister Jeanne. It turned out that the toe had become too infected to be saved, and it would have to be removed. But the infection had spread to the left side of his foot, and that part of the foot would have to be removed also. During this time in the hospital, he contracted sepsis. For those of you who are not familiar with sepsis, it's an infection that needs to be treated right away, or it can attack your heart, and death would be imminent. The doctors were able to cure him of this, and Vito would have to go through many weeks of rehab. A skin graft was planned for the left side of his foot, but it had never gotten good enough for it to happen. I'd go visit him at the rehab center, and we'd talk some, watch a Cubs game, or something; but he could never get his mind off the loss of Joanne. He missed his dog at home, his son, and his granddaughter. Sometimes I'd go with him to the exercise room or the fine motor function exercise room, but I could see the struggle for him, and he just didn't have it in him to be that tough guy that I knew. It was extremely hard to see him in this state of mind. Again he would contract sepsis, and they took him to the hospital where the doctor would treat it again. But Vito refused the treatment and told them to just take him back to the rehab center. The doctor explained to him that if it wasn't treated now, he'd die within a week. Vito just didn't have anymore fight left after months of hospital and rehab centers; he'd had enough.

One morning, a nurse at the rehab center helped him to the bathroom in his room there. She came back to help him out and found him sitting in his wheelchair dead. The doctor was right, not even a week had passed.

So very sad to see my older tough brother that I grew up with and looked up to. Angel number 9 had gone to join the others.

Later in 2018, on September 1, my wife Sandi and I attended a birthday party for one of my students and friend Nikki. It was held at a very nice restaurant in St. Charles, Illinois. There was music, dancing, and several couples attended, including one of my favorite students and dear friend, Julie, and her husband Rob. They sat and hung out with us basically the whole evening. We talked about several things and had a nice time.

Julie knew how much I loved dogs and how I still miss our yellow Lab, so she would post pictures of adoptable dogs on Facebook and tag them to me. This would go on for few years, but one day she posted a picture of this cutest little dog, and I told my wife that after the class at my studio, I wanted to go and meet this cute little dog. Well Sandi wasn't ready to have another dog yet as our yellow Lab was the best there could've ever been. But not knowing that I would call her bluff, she jokingly told me to go ahead, not thinking that I actually would! I had to, it was time to go and meet this little girl!

Once I met her, I knew I couldn't leave her in a kennel any longer; she was a sweet little pup with a look in her eyes that would melt anyone. She was a year and a week old and came on a transport with other dogs from Oklahoma where she had spent some time. I think most of her young life was spent on a concrete floor in confusion. She was very quiet and shy while all the other dogs would be barking and jumping on the front of their kennels. But this little pup just sat there looking at me with this "Please take me home with you" stare. I just couldn't let her sleep and spend her days on a concrete floor ever again.

She's a mix of Australian shepherd and border collie, and I couldn't have found a better, smarter, more intelligent pup! June 24, 2018, I adopted her, and by the suggestion of my dear friend and employee Karen, I named her Liberty. Karen knew I was thinking of a name that would suggest liberation of this little girl. We call her Libby.

During the evening at Nikki's birthday party, somehow the subject of Libby came up as we were sitting at the table with Julie and Rob. As we were talking about her, Sandi had jokingly mentioned to them that if anything were to ever happen to us, Julie would have to take Libby to live with them as it was because of her post to me that we now have Libby. We all laughed about it.

We left the party and drove off a few minutes after Julie and Rob. We took the same route as they did, but they must've made the green lights ahead of us, and we didn't. When we got to a road called Red Gate Road, we had to cross a bridge, which goes from Route 25 over the Fox River, to Route 31. It's maybe a quarter of a mile long, about five or six years old I think—a very nice bridge with sidewalks and large, very strong guardrails. As I turned onto the bridge, we had gone a few hundred feet, and that's when we saw him. He had glanced off the guardrail and was heading toward us at a high speed. He was driving an oversized four-door pickup truck, and glancing off the guardrail changed the direction of his vehicle.

I knew I had to act fast. I came to an immediate stop, hoping that he would avoid hitting us as he came across the road. But within the few seconds it took for all of this to happen, I told Sandi to brace herself. He then slammed into my car. Thank God for the person who invented the seatbelt and airbags. The seatbelts tightened up, and the airbags deployed immediately. As we were pushed backward what was estimated to be at least seventy feet while the car was being turned, there was nothing but darkness and noise from debris and his engine still revving.

I'll never forget the screams from Sandi, "Oh my god," over and over again. As we finally came to a stop after what seemed to be five minutes, or at least that's what it seemed like, my car was sideways with the back end facing the curb. He had flipped over my car, catching the front driver's side of my roof and landed right side up between the back end of my car and the guardrail. It completely blew out the rear window of my car and demolished my trunk. The accident report had given an estimated speed at time of impact of eighty miles per hour, and we were told that we survived by a few seconds of my slamming on my brakes and then keeping both feet on the brake pedal the whole time.

Fortunately, there was a very nice couple, Dan and Michelle, who were witness to the whole ordeal, and they saw him run the red light and his erratic driving. They had phoned the police prior to him slamming into us to report his speeding and erratic driving. They had witnessed the whole accident and what unfolded ahead of them. Thanks to their extreme kindness and caring, the police were already en route, so it wasn't long before they would arrive on the scene. Dan had stopped the guy from trying to escape on foot, and Michelle took photos of the scene. Dan had also helped Sandi out of the car. He tried to help me, but I was stuck and would have to wait for the paramedics to arrive.

We had sustained some injuries, but thankfully nothing life-threatening. The policeman said we were very fortunate that we were not seriously injured or even killed, and that he had never seen anyone survive a crash this bad and walk away with just the injuries we sustained. I got a fracture and a torn ligament in my right hand and several contusions from the seat belt. Sandi suffered three fractured ribs, a sprained ankle, and a slightly punctured lung. A few seconds sooner, and it could've been much worse for us.

He was an eighteen-year-old drunk driver who sustained no injuries but almost killed two people.

Sandi had been by my side through every operation I've had and then through this terrible accident. I believe that guardian angels can exist in a living form. I believe Sandi is my guardian angel in living form; we needed all the guardian angels' help on this night.

Recoveries from my injuries to my hand and wrist took several weeks of rehab after healing, and Sandi's took several months. Luckily, we had Libby to cheer us up at home! We're so very glad that Julie didn't get the opportunity to take Libby. Sandi and I wear glasses, and we both had them knocked off of our faces at some point. When I was able to recover them some days later when my son Jason drove me to the tow yard, neither pair of glasses had a single scratch on them!

Since I wasn't allowed to drive and my painting and teaching hand was disabled for a while, Julie offered to drive out of her way to pick me up and drive me to the studio to see everyone and to see that Karen was doing her fantastic job covering my classes like she had done so many times in the past. Then Julie would drive me home. She's a very caring and loyal friend. Occasionally, Karen would drive me home too—two of my best friends.

Do guardian angels need a few seconds warning of an impending tragedy in order to intervene?

Do guardian angels exist in living form? Sandi was present with me in every circumstance except for the near drowning in boot camp.

Some people may say that I've been lucky through every experience I've been through and that I've had some great surgeons. That would be true. I have had great surgeons, but I feel that I've also been extremely fortunate in the sense that my guardian angels have always been there for me when I needed them the most, I've been told that I'm like a cat who has nine lives. Thanks to all of my guardian angels, I have four left.

ABOUT THE AUTHOR

I've been married to the most wonderful woman who has always been by my side through all of the experiences you'll read in my book, and more for the past forty-nine years, and we have two of the most caring, loving children, Tammy and Jason, who have very wonderful children of their own. Raised Catholics, we believe in our faith and we believe in guardian angels.

I've always been a hardworking man, and when I turned fifty years old, I embarked on a new career. I bought the art studio and have been teaching painting and drawing to adults and children for the past nineteen years.

It's been a mentally rewarding career, and has given me a sense of purpose by helping so many adults and children to get the feeling of great satisfaction, to see the smiles on their faces, when they complete their projects.

I've had many ups and downs over the years, but I've always kept the faith, as I'm sure many of you have also. I hope you will enjoy reading my book.